Stock Trading:

This book includes:

- *Swing Trading*
- *Swing Trading Strategies*

Swing Trading:

The Ultimate Guide to Making
Fast Money 1 Hour a Day

The information in the following pages is broadly considered to be a truthful and accurate account of facts and as such any inattention, use or misuse of the information in question by the reader will render any resulting actions solely under their purview. There are no scenarios in which the publisher or the original author of this work can be, in any fashion, deemed liable for any hardship or damages that may befall them after undertaking information described herein.

Additionally, the information in the following pages is intended only for informational purposes and should thus be thought of as universal. As befitting its nature, it is presented without assurance regarding its prolonged validity or interim quality. Trademarks are mentioned without written consent and can in no way be considered an endorsement from the trademark holder.

Table of Contents

Introduction

Congratulations on downloading '*Swing Trading: The Ultimate Guide to Making Fast Money 1 Hour a Day,*' and thank you for doing so.

The following chapters will discuss what swing trading on the market is and how you can get the most out of it by using the right strategies. When it comes to making a trade, there are a lot of things to consider and this book will help you get into details about every aspect needed to take conscious and smart decisions.

There are plenty of books on this subject on the market, so thanks again for choosing this one! Every effort was made to ensure it is full of as much useful information as possible, please enjoy!

Chapter 1: Understanding Swing Trading—the Differences Between Swing Trading, Day Trading, and Buy-and-Hold Investing

Have you ever heard the word 'swing trading' before? But have you ever understood what it really means? It's actually quite simple: it means making your money work while you do whatever it is that you want. Basically, it's a different way of thinking that you can use to make money. Growing up, most of us have been taught that we can only earn an income by finding a good job. And that's exactly what most of us do. But there is a big problem in this, if you want more money, you have to work longer hours. However, there is a limit to the number of hours a day we can work on, not to mention the fact that having a lot of money is somewhat meaningless if we do not have the time to enjoy it. This is why rich people do not have a job because they have the businesses that do the work for them.

Think about it, you have a job that allows you to earn over 2000 euros a month, but that takes you over 13 hours a day, 6 days out of 7, so about 11 remain and of course you need to take at least 7-8 hours of sleep (for a healthy lifestyle) then you need to consider the displacements and the time spent so you can reach work, you will only have 3-4 hours of free time remaining, most likely you will use 2 of those remaining free hours for dinner in the evening. In the end, you actually have 2 hours of free time per day. This is not enough for you to enjoy life to the fullest. You find yourself having a salary of 2000 euros a month (which nowadays is worth almost nothing with the increase in expenditures) that will just continue to accumulate and you absolutely won't have the time to enjoy them in any way as you will spend most of your waking hours trying to earn more. This is what most people would call the 'rat race.'

Is there a solution? Yes, it exists, and it is to take a part of your money and invest it properly in the financial markets, and letting it do the work for you. The possibilities are scary and risks are definitely involved but this can be extremely profitable. One example? Apple's stocks.

Apple stocks have risen at a frightening rate in the last 10 years, from $10 to about 100. This means that with an investment of only $ 1,000, you would now have over 10 thousand dollars. This is the power of online investments, it allows your money to grow in a completely automatic way.

Unfortunately, you can't do the same at work by having a duplicate finish your tasks, but instead, you can create an extension of yourself—that is your money—and put it to work. In this way, while you are busy burning away the hours at work, or while you are at the bar hanging out with friends, you can earn and make profits at the same time thanks to the investment you made. Put simply, you can expand your horizon through the effective application of your money and maximize your potential to earn even if you do not receive an increase in your pay, or even if you decide not to make an extraordinary one or if you are looking for a more beneficial job.

What is 'swing trading?' How does the

swing trading technique work? These are two of the questions that inexperienced traders can ask themselves. In fact, swing trading is, together with 'Day trading' and 'Buy and Hold trading,' one of the most commonly known ways to invest. This is why many traders pick this method to do their trading, it's already tried and proven. This manner of trade is the intermediate version between 'Buy and Hold' and 'Day Trading.'

Anyone who wants to try Forex trading, whether he is a novice trader or a market expert, must decide on which trading technique they'll want to use.

Swing trading is one of the most widespread and effective techniques, this trading method is also characterized by many aspects that facilitate its practice. So you can invest in this approach even if you do not have much experience.

The decision to follow the technique of swing trading, rather than another, precedes the actual operational phase and depends strictly on the preferences of the trader and the type of approach he or she wants to pursue.

To have a quick review of the basics, there are mainly three different trading techniques, as we have already mentioned. These types are classified on the basis of the reference time horizon:

- Intraday trading: open a position and close it within the day

- Swing trading: open a position and close it after a few or a few days

- Buy and hold trading: open a

position and close it after weeks or months

Swing trading is, therefore, the most flexible method of trading, which tries to balance the defects of other, more extreme methods. A method that takes the best of both worlds and tries to eliminate the greater problems which are found in the other methods.

After seeing what 'scalping is,' an extreme declination of intraday trading, we now understand exactly what are the advantages offered by the swing trading technique and begin to analyze its differences from the other main techniques.

Swing trading is an easy-to-learn trading technique that engages novice traders and more experienced traders, without taking up too much time or the fun hidden in trading. Swing trading, is in fact, that trading technique that allows you to open a position on Forex, short or long, and close it from there after a few days, capturing the sentiment of the change and the swing described in that situation.

The trend of a price follows the continuous swing, downward or upward, which may last one or more market days. There is, therefore, no fixed price, but your position adapts to price fluctuations. In fact, those who work with this method are really aiming for this price swing.

The swing trader is the one who identifies these oscillations and 'rides the wave' for a variable period of time, which is neither too short to limit the gains nor too long to risk the inversion. In other words, it takes advantage of the favorable trend of the moment for a short period of time, before moving on to the next opportunity of making a profit. Swing trading strategies can be carried out in a very different time frame, which can range from a few days to whole months. This will depend very much on the person's trading style since each one will opt for a different timing.

Forex is the ideal market to practice swing trading because primarily it is extremely fluid and full of traders. The result will be the description of trends with continuous oscillations, which will rely on the skill of the trader to fully grasp.

How do swing traders make decisions?

Technical analysis is important in forming a swing trading strategy because it is fundamental that you are able to identify the moment when a corrective movement can end and when you can trade in the direction of the prevailing trend, increasing the chances of achieving success. In conclusion, technical analysis can help you clearly identify entry levels.

Furthermore, many swing traders base their strategies on macroeconomic issues. This means that if, for example, a war in an oil-producing country breaks out, this increases the chances that the price of oil will increase. In this scenario, a trader could aim to go long on the oil, expecting that this event could affect market prices over the next two weeks. The identification of the topics is of great help in trading because very often the events that occur around us help us to evaluate the sentiment on the different financial markets.

Can I swing trade against the trend?

Some swing traders tend to trade against the trend but does this mean that their chances of making a profit are therefore lower? Not always, as an important part of swing trading is the 'multi-timeframe' analysis. This means that a trader does not analyze a single time frame on the graph but makes his decisions based on the analysis of multiple intervals.

As an example, suppose that the daily interval indicates an increasing trend. In contrast, the hourly and fifteen-minute intervals may indicate that a decrementing movement could begin in the short and medium term. In this case, the trader knows that even if the long-term trend is on the upside, he can still make profits in the short or medium term using the signals generated by the shorter time intervals.

Chapter 2: Pros and Cons — the Costs and Benefits of Swing Trading

How much should be traded today?

Another important point before starting the practice of swing trading is to understand how much you are willing to invest today. The amount of capital that you are willing to invest changes not only because of the trader's economic resources but also because of the degree of preparation.

For this reason, we consider it useful to advise you to start investing with a demo account, or a free trading account, which allows you to understand what the risks of online trading are, but above all to feel the trading strategies or even just gain additional knowledge while you practice with the trading platform. Given this, let's examine how much should be put in an investment today.

Swing trading capital today requires:
- The possibility of making use of its capital

- Use of financial resources in fruit-bearing operations

How much is the capital needed to start swing trading today?

There are many traders who associate the meaning of a large sum of money to the term 'capital.' Obviously, not everyone will agree on how much a capital should be exactly, but every trader decides to invest his capital, according to the possibilities or opportunities. So, for a basic level trader, investing €100 is equivalent to an experienced trader investing €1000.

Capital, therefore, is a relative amount for each of us. Almost always, however, capital, in its most general meaning, takes the form of a value that is very difficult to obtain and use for a possible investment.

Today we can tell you exactly how the world of online trading has become accessible to everyone, even to traders who do not have immense amounts of capital.

How much do you need to trade for tangible results?

There are brokers that offer the possibility of investing in the stock market even with only €100 of initial capital, a ridiculous amount, which allows you not only to experience the world of online investments but also to get rid of the baseless assumption that online trading or Stock exchange investments are only for those who own a lot of money. This is what I call a 'test capital.'

To understand this concept, we must consider it to be of fundamental importance; if one understands it, the very concept of capital takes on a different meaning; in fact, it will mean every definition of greatness or importance. In other words, the concept of capital will mean only the amount of money that is available and in the case of wrong investment does not affect the overall financial situation of the trader.

Be careful not to confuse this with the concept of carelessly investing money. In reverse! You will have to treat the money you plan to invest with the utmost respect and always keep its importance in mind. Just constantly remind yourself that you earned that money by working hard and you do not want to waste it.

Remember that investing in online trading is risky because of the possibility of losing the entire capital. So pay close attention to this concept. It does not matter what the amount to invest, or what capital is available! The important thing is to understand the value of the capital that you're planning to invest.

If you follow our advice, you can find out how easy and quick it is to do online trading or invest in the stock market with just a few steps, and especially like all of this today, is really affordable for everyone thanks to the internet. There is nothing left but to continue this path and make the information in this guide yours so you can learn how to invest today.

Understanding that investments must earn money for those who invest in them is a fundamental concept. Although it may seem rather trivial, not knowing where to invest is and above all, not the same idea. Understanding which sectors to bet on is not trivial!

There are 2 possible ways to invest money. Investing money also means making that money do the work for you and that is why you should invest money in the first place. In fact, we all know and understand that money is one of the major components of having a modern life. Money serves and is the basis of a myriad of fundamental activities that belong to our lives.

The 2 roads to follow are divided between:

- Having the money

- Using the money

To better explain these concepts, let's give an example. It is common for people to say: "Put the savings under the mattress." This concept, although quite trivial, teaches us this method that can make us owners of a certain sum of money in the future.

However, owning money does not require any investment. In order for money to bring great yields, it must be invested. The money must, therefore, be used, or invested, not just held. This is especially true when considering the constant loss of value cash undergoes every year because of inflation. Investing can be seen as a way to betting against money itself and this is what I tend to think about when considering an opportunity.

How can a capital be used to invest?

Various uses of money include shopping, buying consumer goods, a new smartphone, a new car, or even other consumer goods. But there is more to using money than fulfilling our basic needs or material wants.

Even having a small amount of money deposited in the bank or other fields, can't be considered wrong. In all these cases, money is invested and yields. This is the concept of using money to make more money and it is precisely the concept of investing today.

If you use the money as your investment funds it is quite certain it's being used to make more money. In this case, producing money does not require much effort and additional initiative on your part. We only have to hope that the markets we have invested in are always positive, that is, they always close with a gain for us. Of course, it does not mean that you can just forget about it, deciding where and how your money should be invest will always fall on to you.

To do this, you can rely on financial magnates or choose to invest in online trading or other markets thanks to online brokers, who can offer you a complete training on the markets and online trading, which will then allow you to invest your money and strategize accordingly to make the right choices.

By taking these training courses, you will be aware of some theoretical and technical factors. The more information you have, the greater the chances of earning for you.

Swing trading money today: 2 ways to swing trade

We can divide the investments into 2 big categories:

- Buy something, wait for its value to increase, and then resell it at a higher value so that you can make a decent profit. In this case, most investors buy and sell real estate.

- Investing by buying shares. In this case, the investor becomes the owner of a piece of the company for which he has taken out an action, with the hope that the value of the stock will rise so that he can then sell his stock to a new buyer or shareholder, and collect the profit.

At the moment, I will focus more on this last aspect, as I consider it the most developed and as this will certainly a greater and more diverse portfolio.

Investing in the stock market today is also possible thanks to 'options trading.' Basically, 'options trading' makes it possible to invest in shares and also earn from a decreased value. Buying this type of financial instrument, allows you to earn even if the overall value goes down.

Another widely used strategy to invest today and to capitalize on its capacity to lend money for a certain period of time and then receive it with interest. Today we will talk a lot about this sector and especially about bond investments.

What is the minimum capital that you need to swing trade?

This is one of the most recurring questions that are asked by people who would like to start and eventually dedicate themselves to this activity. The answer, as we shall see, depends on many factors and in this chapter I would like to clarify some aspects that affect the choice of initial capital.

Let's start immediately by saying that the amount we decide to allocate to the trading activity, whatever the objective we want to achieve, must not be a capital we need to supply our daily needs. It must be, as I like to call it, an 'available capital'.

In other words, since investing is a risky activity (and so it's trading), like any other financial transaction, the money we devote to trading if lost, must not, in any way, affect the status of our financial stability greatly.

The question we must ask is, if we lose the money we have decided to dedicate to investing, do we compromise our family's livelihood in any way? If yes, you can either reduce the amount up to the parameters of 'tranquillity' or avoid dedicating yourselves to this activity, at least until you are in a position to have a decent capital available that meets the minimum requirements.

Recently I happened to meet a gentleman who, wanting to follow my own course during a discounted 'launch' offer to start trading using my system, asked me if I could keep the offer for a few days, to give him time to release his savings invested in accumulation plans in his bank. Since those were his only (and small) savings, I calmly advised him to let go of the course and the real operation, at least for the moment, and in the meantime to focus on studying while waiting for better opportunities (read: pending to have an 'available capital.') This I think should be the philosophy of all those who want to devote to what is defined by many as one of the most beautiful professions one can dedicate themselves to.

After this first 'rock' we try to understand what is the minimum capital we should devote to trading. Which, as we said at the beginning, depends on many factors. Unfortunately, the current generation which was exposed to trading for the first is the result of misleading advertisements that exaggerated the achievement of incredible wealth or earning incredibly large sums from starting with just a few hundred euros.

Although it is true that with the advent of CFDs—which offer an excellent leverage on almost all financial instruments—and cryptocurrencies (which, in some cases like Ripple made over 16,000% in 2017) today it is possible to trade with just a few hundred euros, it is clear that we can't immediately become rich from investing a small amount of capital, or less likely, to have a lucrative extra monthly income.

Instead, we can reasonably think, so to speak, of 'biting ourselves' on real markets by acquiring the necessary experience. Only once we have obtained stable results, we will be able to use more capital and aim to have an extra monthly income to add to our income from work (which, in the meantime, I absolutely advise not to abandon).

So let's say we start to put stakes: if we have an 'available capital' that is around €500, this amount can be enough to start if and only if, our goal is to check our ability to trade and to determine if we can achieve constantly positive results. In other words, it can be seen as a 'testing capital,' used to gather experience rather than profits.

But beware, we must not run the risk of using exaggerated leverage. This means that we will have to open up transactions (and CFDs give us this opportunity) with very small lots and be content with small gains (and have small losses). Otherwise, using maximum leverage, we would risk burning the amount instantly with just a very few transactions. If you want, you can go further into the topic in my article on leverage.

If the objective is to have an extra monthly income instead, then the amount that should be allocated to trading (and we always talk about 'available capital' in the indicated sense) must be at least 3,000 to 5,000 euros. Of course, the operation cannot always be dedicated to instruments such as CFDs because it would be unthinkable, with this amount capital, to operate on different instruments that require margins far higher than those required by CFDs.

With 3000 to 5000 euros—of course, once you have acquired the necessary experience and a reliable trading method—we can set ourselves the goal of having an extra income that is around 200 or 300 euros per month, maintaining a low-risk profile. They might seem a bit small and dissatisfying, but if we consider the percentage return on 'risk capital', it is a respectable ratio.

Advantages of swing trading

From all that has been said up until now, the advantages of this trading technique are clear. Operating through swing trading offers one the opportunity to manage their profits, with the aim of maximizing them over time without incurring risks of achieving unpleasant losses. Excellent in managing the stress, as it does not involve having to follow in a frantic and anxious manner unlike with intraday trading. The position is in fact held over several days and this 'spreads' anxiety in the right way.

Swing trading also allows you to settle. We have seen how those who work through buy and hold trading are likely to run into the situation of trying to widen their earning prospects as much as possible, given the few operations carried out. With swing trading, however, the goal is to focus on a part of the bullish or bearish movement, without having to buy on a minimum level or sell on a maximum level and thus, making a profit as a result.

Disadvantages of swing trading

But it is not all sunshine and roses. Like all things, this technique also has its disadvantages. In fact, this technique requires a fair study of the market and the meticulous creation of a strategy. Then, however, the losses are more consistent compared to day trading and generally turns out to be more boring because it is less adrenaline pumping than the other methods that take place all in one day.

How much can you earn?

The questions of people who aim to invest in stocks have always remained the same from the day the stock market was born and I would like to respond to these in depth. Example queries:

- How much do you earn in the stock market?

- How to start playing in the stock market?

- How do you earn on the Forum Exchange?

- How much can you earn by investing in the stock market?

- I lost everything in the bag

The last one will seem strange, but it is one of the many searches that many users make. They are traders who lose their investment on the stock exchange and we should try not to make the same mistakes by studying the financial markets and investing with a non-high risk profile and a diversified portfolio.

An investor will always ask how much you earn by choosing to swing trade in the stock market and it's not quite easy to give this question a specific answer. Most professional traders, in fact, know perfectly well that the amount of gain that can be obtained on the stock exchange is also linked to subjective factors. It is these latter that really determine what is then called a 'gain.'

The return on an investment in the stock exchange is also linked to a series of elements restricted over time. Investing today on the stock market is certainly not the same way it was 10 years ago. In fact, back then, it was in full expansion. The FTSE MIB had reached very high levels and the performance of the individual shares seemed to increase continuously.

That era has been over officially for some time. Investing in the stock market today means exposing yourself to various risks that weren't present a decade ago. Entire sectors of the stock market, such as the banking sector, are not the only sectors subject to a seemingly unstoppable price erosion. This is another element to take into consideration when trying to understand how much you can earn on the stock market. Compared to the past, investing today in the stock market means being aware of the fact that there are securities whose relaunch still seems very far away.

All the factors listed belong to the determination of how much you earn with the stock exchange. It is a variable sum linked to contingencies. But is there a way to calculate when to invest in the stock exchange and when not to? In other words, is it possible to determine a minimum sum above which the investment was successful?

The minimum gain that can be obtained on the stock exchange and can be considered a successful investment is the result of a kind of summation. By removing the field from possible misunderstandings it is always important to highlight that the factors that need to be added do not concern the subjective sphere of the investor. Instead, these are purely objective elements.

The first, and most important, concerns inflation. When choosing to buy stocks, it is hoped that, at the end of the investment, the increased capital will not be lost with the increase in the consumer price index. Now it is clear that, when starting to invest in the stock market, the inflation rate is not known but only reputable. During the investment, however, we have all the information available to quantify what would have been the natural increase in the amount invested in light of the trend of inflation.

This makes it possible to get an accurate picture of the change in the consumer price index year after year.

Assuming that there are zero risk investments on the market (a postulate rather than a reality), investing in the stock market is worthwhile if the yield is higher than that which is obtainable with the risk-free security. To do this calculation you can take into consideration the government bonds of a highly developed country. The yields of these bonds, clearly low, must then be compared with those of the investment on the stock exchange.

The interest rate that is paid by this risk-free security must, therefore, be added to the index relating to the trend in consumer prices. Thus we obtain a first data which, however, is still incomplete.

To determine exactly what is the expected gain of the investment on the stock exchange, a third element must be added. At this point, one enters the field of subjectivity. The third variable is an additional margin that compensates for the risk taken by the investor. Quantifying this third element is not at all simple. Traders, however, are used to quantifying the risk run in a couple of percentage points.

The definitive summation to determine how much you earn by choosing to invest in the stock market can be summarized as follows: inflation + return on capital + additional margin. In total, it's around 11 percentage points.

The 11 percentage points of return obtainable by investing in the stock market are gross. It is, therefore, necessary to subtract all the items of expenditure, including taxes. Furthermore, this is a level that is supported by a normal trend in the consumer price index. It is obvious, on the other hand, that today with low inflation, that minimum level tends to fall further. The summation alone, however, provides a partial picture of how much money should be earned 'at a minimum' on the stock exchange.

A very important factor is the duration of the investment. In this case, the rule is very clear: to obtain interesting returns, hold shares for very long periods. This happened over 10 years ago. In fact, at the time, economic growth seemed to be unlimited and the trend in inflation was positive too. In those years, the same stock indexes improved continuously. But that picture has failed today.

Paradoxically, to make an earning on the stock exchange, based on the model mentioned, you would have to go back more than ten years.

All the major analysts say that investing today in the stock market makes sense only if the shares can be maintained for 10 years. It takes time to succeed, so, year after year, to accrue an interesting return. But over time it also serves a lot of confidence in a restart.

The example of banking sector securities is just the tip of an iceberg of what is happening on the stock exchange. If you look at the prices of the many stocks in recent years, you notice the total absence of lasting restart. It is true that this situation has been taking root especially in recent years, but who says that the picture will improve in a few years? This is the real breaking point compared to the past.

Today the balance of risks or opportunities hang, and not a little, on the first course. The factors to be taken into consideration are many starting from systemic risk. The stock market trend, in fact, has to deal with the macro framework of reference and it is pitiless. The global economic recovery, in fact, does not take off.

Going down to the domestic market, the underlying picture is even more deteriorated. For this reason alone, investing in Italian shares is already a less advantageous step than an investment in US equities. All reports of the International Monetary Fund do not leave much hope in this regard, the difficult situation is bound to last in the future.

The overall risk is then increased as further elements of concern have been inserted into this framework. The examples, in this sense, are the Brexit but also the serious crisis faced by Italian banks.

Therefore, investing in long-term stocks remains a bet for strong hearts. The fact that the long-term risks have increased, however, does not mean that it is impossible to gain on the stock market today. There is a way to avoid being overwhelmed by these fears. The road is to focus on the short term. The means to travel this way is to rely on binary trading and Forex & CFD Trading.

Alongside the various factors that we have mentioned as elements of risk to be reckoned with by choosing to invest in the stock market today, there are also purely economic considerations that advise against the long term. That 11% we have indicated as the minimum sum that can be earned, in fact, is gross. In that percentage, in fact, various expenses are charged that derive from being a shareholder.

Those who choose to buy shares are subject to a series of taxes and are obliged to respect a lot of duties. It is obvious that if this happens at a time of financial expansion then it is not a problem. On the other hand, if it starts at a time of crisis, then it is a crucial factor that discourages the long term.

Investing today on the stock exchange means relying on 'Binary trading' and 'CFD trading.' In fact, only these two financial instruments make it possible to obtain a profit that is not subject to the many risks of the long term. With binary options and 'Contracts for Difference,' it is possible to bet on the progress of a stock even for very short time intervals.

This is especially true in the case of binary options. Investing in the stock market with options trading means betting on which direction that our action will take in the short time of 60 seconds following the opening of the trade. It is obvious that if the mechanism of operation of binary options is this, then all the talk about the risks of long-term investment makes no sense.

Options trading, on the other hand, is a way to defend against the high uncertainty that is ultimately characterizing the markets.

These same considerations apply in the

case of CFD trading. The latter very closely resembles the traditional purchase of shares. With CFD trading it is possible to buy instruments that are linked to the performance of specific actions. You earn and lose in relation to the trend of listing but with a substantial difference compared to the stock exchange.

In fact, when you buy CFD, you do not charge any duty. Also, the expenses of a commission are certainly not like those of the shares. Earnings, on the other hand, can be immediate. In this case, too, short-term investments can be carried out.

But where can you trade online today? In recent years there has been a boom in authorized platforms. This covered both binary trading and CFD trading. The list below shows the best brokers to earn trading with the stock market. It is good to remember that the use of these instruments can lead to the loss of capital. For this reason, before betting on online trading, it is always better to practice on demo platforms. These allow simulating the trading activity without risking losses.

All the best trading platforms give this opportunity that can be exercised without time limits. By joining the practice on the trading platform and a study on technical analysis and fundamental analysis, it is possible to create a valid alternative to the investment on the stock exchange. How much you earn today with online trading is definitely higher than what you earn on the stock market. Testing with a demo account costs nothing. Today, however, the role of inflation has become secondary. The curve of consumer price trends leaves no room for misunderstanding. Inflation is increasing nowadays slowly and indeed, the risk of deflation hides around the corner. This is why we need to consider other elements to define and determine what we can earn today in the stock market.

Chapter 3: Risks and Common Mistakes to Avoid—the Specific Risks That Come With Swing Trading and How to Avoid Common Mistakes

The risks of swing trading regardless of the type of platform you'll choose can be divided into 3 different categories:

- Scam risk

- Risk on capital

- Psychological risk

For decades, the top experts in trading and then later on online trading, have become engrossed in these issues trying to find a solution to mitigate or eliminate the effects of risk on trading. Fortunately today we have reached excellent conclusions and great progress has been made in terms of prevention and management of all types of risk that are related to trading activity. If you also want to become a successful trader you need to know the risks of your professional activity to be able to take the necessary countermeasures.

Welcome to our guide, which you can use to pursue your career and earn well in the field of online trading. We now proceed by analyzing the type of risks and propose a possible solution.

Scam Risk

We can consider ourselves lucky because we write in a particularly quiet time regarding the scams in trading and more generally, online scams. For a long time now the network has spread widely on our territory as well as worldwide, so the authorities are organized to defend users of the internet and protect them from scams. In Italy, there is a very efficient postal police that regulates and enforces the law on most of the types of scams used on the network, while in the field of financial instruments and products in our country, CONSOB is particularly vigilant.

About ten years ago when this sector experienced its first real expansion, in fact, there were documented cases of scams of all kinds, there were even 'puppet sites' that were dismantled immediately after making fun of a few thousand users, robbing their deposits, but today, fortunately, the situation has radically changed, of course in a positive sense! Since online trading has become extremely popular and has become widespread, it's not an activity which can be abandoned and ignored, the authorities have taken the necessary steps towards establishing complete and total regulation today, an excellent result that secures all of the traders who make their investments online.

Council for the risk of fraud

This is the riskless 'heavy' because now it is very easy to avoid. It is sufficient to inquire well before registering and making a deposit, on the reliability of the broker. The names of the best brokers for online trading are known all too well and you will have no difficulty in finding them to immediately start on your trading activity protected by law, but also by the high-quality service that the best brokers today are able to offer: low minimum deposits, secure accounts, encrypted personal data, fast withdrawals and platforms with real-time data that cannot be tampered with. The risk of fraud is ultimately null if you choose official brokers and regulated by authorities such as CONSOB and CYSEC, in this case, there is absolutely no risk and you can operate in maximum safety

We talked about avoiding unreliable brokers without a CYSEC license. These platforms are a danger even if you actually made some money. In fact, there are sites that allow you to make deposits without problems in a few minutes by bank transfer or credit card. The bad surprise comes however when you want to withdraw your money. The operation will be hindered in every way, for example by asking for documents that cannot be provided or other devices to prevent profits from being taken home. If asked, the customer service will no longer be heard, the phone remains unanswered and the messages will be ignored. These are the signs of a typical scam. Unreliable payment processes are one of the most frequent fraud methods used by unreliable brokers.

Risk on Capital

Once you have deposited your capital with an authorized broker you must also avoid wasting it. Although online trading represents the business to be carried out on the net with the best prospects of absolute profit, about 80% of traders lose all their capital in a short amount of time. This happens because beginners underestimate the risk of loss and very often even those who already have a certain degree of experience do so.

Trading online means investing and an

investment activity has two sides of the same coin. An investment can go wonderfully well, but it can also go terribly wrong. The traders, therefore, have the objective of making their income and expenses equally balanced, maximizing the opportunities for profit and limiting their losses as much as possible.

Losing is normal, there is no trader in the world who doesn't lose, even the best traders suffer losses from time to time, the important thing is that they are limited, contained and managed in the best possible ways. So no need for a hysterical crisis, dear trader, all you need is to be aware and operate the management of your capital wisely. Even if your losses are quite high, you can always recover thanks to the remaining capital, which however must now be invested with strict criteria in consideration to get the better of the adverse, poorly reasoned or unfortunate phases of your career.

Tips for managing capital risks

To teach capital risk management techniques you would have to write entire books on the subject, there are just so many tips and techniques at your disposal, so do not worry, all you have to do is inform yourself properly and you'll always see your capital grow and your balance of profits increase. To rationalize then act, this is the key to success in an activity like online trading, where not only do you gain but also exposes you to risks. Your trading must be planned with every possible detail in mind. You must look at your initial capital and divide it into a series of low-risk operations.

Imagine that the amount of your risk

based on available capital is 100%, you must know that you have the freedom to break this amount and choose how much to risk for each trade based on the money you invest. If you commit your entire capital, which for example we will imagine amounting to € 1,000, in a single trading operation, in that case, your risk on the capital would be 100%! This means that if your operation goes wrong you will lose everything you have! At that point, it would be a very hard blow, but this does not have to happen and there is an obvious solution to the problem.

To avoid losing everything you have, you need to invest little or very little for every order you send to the market. You must never risk more than 2-5% of your total capital for each trade so at that point you can be sure that even if the operation goes horribly wrong, you have lost almost nothing, but if you have invested successfully you made a profit, that added to others can lead your account to increase significantly step by step consistently over time.

Psychological risk

Another very present risk, but also very underestimated by traders is the risk linked to the psychology of online trading. The risk in trading can in fact also arise from factors of emotional origin, a fact that too often we tend to forget and not calculate, but a microscopic error is actually committed. All the most experienced traders know how much the psychological factor counts in trading, it is so strong that it's even considered one of the main engines in the market.

Since you only represent a small cell in the great cauldron of the financial markets, the psychological risk is a purely individual fact but it must be dealt with effectively regardless. For example, very often it can happen if you suddenly make big gains by investing in online trading. You may think that this is good, but actually, it's bad. This great advantage often turns into a problem especially for traders without experience because it leads us to think that earnings are raining from the sky and are not the result of a reasoned and organized activity.

Council for psychological risk

A secret of professionals in the sector lies in knowing how to remain impassive and controlled in front of every event. The most experienced traders know how to remain impassive and stoic even in the face of unfortunate days with huge losses because they know that times will change and the chance for triumph will come.

The experienced trader will always remain absolutely calm even before big entrances because losing their calm or concentration will lead them to start thinking they're invincible and fully capable of dominating all the markets would be a very serious mistake that can result in impulsive and hasty decisions. If these are the effects on an experienced trader think about what happens to a beginner, a 'victim' of all these emotional upheavals related to the loss or to the earnings of money. The most important thing is to keep a cold state of mind and maintain a logical approach to everything.

Risk, as well as profit, is one of the essential aspects of online trading. Although it is a reality that must not be hidden and which cannot be avoided, every prudent trader has the possibility to manage it and adopt all the necessary countermeasures in order to obtain great profits and a sparkling success in this exciting activity. Managing risk is not impossible, you just have to learn how to do it. Once you learn how to choose a broker, how to manage capital, and how to control (and never repress) your emotions, all goals become attainable and real.

Chapter 4: Examples—a Few Brief Examples of How to Begin Swing Trading, As Well As Resources and Navigating Data

We have already spoken extensively about how to swing trade in the stock market and how this activity can generate very high profits. Precisely because of a large number of profits that can be obtained and this is also why many people aspire to become stock traders. But how do you learn to invest in the stock market?

The point is that the exchange is not a game. Every time someone uses the term 'play in the stock market' that means they're going down the wrong path because it is not a game, it is about investment. The best way to learn how to invest in the stock exchange is to start investing with an intuitive and easy-to-use broker. The best solution in my opinion? Definitely 24option. Among other things, those who register at 24option also get free excellent trading alerts to know where it's easier to invest in the stock markets.

Swing trading from home

The first characteristic of the swing trade in the stock market that is immediately noticed by the eye is that it is an investment that can be made directly from home. It is no longer necessary to go to the Bank to hand over the purchase orders to the employee on duty. Old traders feel nostalgic when they remember those bank branches that had become a bit of a meeting place for the 'Oxen Park,' given a large number of traders who met and exchanged information and observations. On one hand, it is a positive thing, since investing in the stock market through an Italian bank is the best way to get skim off commissions and even lose money, given the inadequacy of the tools offered.

The only positive aspect of these 'Oxen Park' meetings was the opportunity of passing on the necessary experience to people who were just starting to invest in the stock market. Learning to invest in the stock market guided by the comments and experiences of older, more experienced traders is something that is difficult to do if you work from home. To solve this problem you have the option to attend discussion forums and try to establish a dialogue with the most experienced users. Though, you must always be very careful in believing what you're told on these forums because not all the information gained is actually true.

Investing in the stock exchange from home, using tools such as binary options or contracts for difference, is much more convenient than going to a bank branch physically.

What are the best platforms to invest in if you want to trade from home? There are few platforms that are truly reliable and affordable. Among the best platforms to invest in the stock exchange, we can report are the following:

- Plus500: safe and reliable, it is a truly professional platform. Plus500 is a 'Contract for Difference (CFD)' trading platform that allows you to invest in thousands of shares listed on all major world markets.

- 24option: a truly safe and reliable binary options broker, perfect for investing in the stock market.

- IQ Option: one of the most innovative binary options brokers. It is very safe and reliable. Offers a free unlimited demo account in time and quantities. IQ Option is the only platform for trading on the stock market that allows you to start investing with just 10 euros.

How to start swing trading in the stock market

The first step to start investing in the stock market is to know what the stock exchange is. It might seem obvious but it's not like that. Many traders start stock trading without even knowing what it is. The stock exchange is the regulated financial market on which shares are exchanged, which represent securities owned by listed companies. Each share gives the right, as the case may be, to receive a dividend (a portion of the company profits that are redistributed) and to participate in the ordinary and extraordinary meetings of a company.

Usually, however, it is not advisable to invest in the stock market through the shares. The best way to start investing in the stock market is to focus on derivative contracts that have underlying shares. In this way, you get the advantage of increasing earnings and, above all, earning both when stocks go down and when they go up when you make the right prediction.

How to learn swing trading on the stock market

At this point, you are probably asking, "How can I learn to play the stock market?" The title of this paragraph is a provocation because we know that we must not talk about gambling but about investing. In any case, how do you start? How do you learn? The best way to start is to have options. These derivative instruments, in fact, are very simple to use and understand. In fact, binary trading is very easy. If we choose a stock listed on a world exchange (one of the main ones, of course) we only have to indicate whether the price of the asset will be increased or decreased at the end of a period of time. It does not count the level of variation, only the sign counts and this is perfect for learning because the aspiring trader can concentrate only on a few fundamental factors, leaving out all the other unnecessary details. It must be said that options trading can produce profits so high that many traders are choosing to trade options only, although they do not need a simplified approach.

How to operate on the stock exchange

We have already seen that in order to operate on the stock exchange it is convenient to use derivative instruments, binary options are better to start with and, later, CFDs can also be adopted (Contracts for Difference).Another important choice to make when investing in the stock exchange, especially at the beginning, is to focus exclusively on the best stocks, i.e. those large, well-known companies listed on the world's major stock exchanges.

Among other things, the major options brokers and CFDs all provide access to the big stocks but not access to smaller listed companies, perhaps they can be found in secondary stock exchanges like the one in Milan. Though, these titles are usually an indicator of extreme danger and the novice trader who decides to choose them might be at serious risk of losing their hard-earned money.

How trades in the stock market work

For a wholesome level of information, I try to make a global overview of the functioning of investments on the stock exchange. In general, it is possible to invest in the stock market with the direct purchase of listed shares or with the purchase of derivatives. In general, for those who have the problem of how to start investing in the stock exchange, the recommended choice is that of derivatives, in particular, binary options. For those who want to buy the securities directly, the process is slightly more complex. You have to open an account for the custody of shares and on this deposit, you, unfortunately, pay a stamp. Moreover, this type of investment usually passes for Italian banks and involves high fees and poor service. Vice versa, for those who choose to invest in the stock market with binary options or CFDs, there are zero commissions and a service that really works very well.

Another way to invest on the stock exchange is through the use of mutual funds. Investments of this type work by purchasing a share of the fund. The managers then use the money obtained through the sale of shares to invest the stock exchanges. This is an indirect investment that delegates all responsibilities to fund managers. In some cases, decent profits can be made, but it has often happened that investment funds, especially if managed by Italian companies, have led to very terrible losses. Moreover, the tax treatment of this type of investment is incredibly penalizing.

Investment strategies

It is much better to do it yourself, then. But when you work with options or CFDs on the stock exchange you need to have investment strategies that you can rely on. In general, we can say that there are very simple strategies that allow us to predict the market trend based on the direct observation of the graphs. It is also possible to predict the market trend based on the news relating to the various listed companies. Finally, for those who wish to delegate the choice of strategies to others without incurring the costs of investment funds, it is always possible to subscribe to trading signals services. In practice, it is another trader (or group of traders) that indicates by e-mail, SMS or integration with the trading platform, what the right transaction is at the right time.

The investment in the medium and long-term is ideal for those who want to build a capital, or simply diversify and increase savings over time at reduced costs. Given their versatility, 'ETFs' can be used in different medium and long-term investment strategies, where they can support or replace traditional instruments, thus allowing the attainment of the set objective. Currently, the range of ETFs is so diverse that any FCI can be replicated (at a much higher cost).

A strategy to swing trade capital in the medium to long term is to resort to investment funds, which has seen a rise in popularity over the last twenty years. One of the main characteristics of the funds is that it allows the underwriter to enter the market with modest capital and to obtain professional management that will help them obtain positive results over time, with a moderate risk. Investment funds should favor more active management, even if this does not always happen. In addition to weighing on their final return, they are the highest management costs to which the same funds are subject, and whose impact is felt particularly in times of slowdown or stagnation of the market. In light of this situation, the investor could find that it is convenient to substitute the investment in funds with that of ETFs that aim to closely follow the evolution of its benchmark index while offering the maximum possible transparency.

In advance it cannot be said whether it is better to invest in funds or in ETF; to make this choice you have to decide if you want the manager to move away from the benchmark (and from which benchmark), this possibility is called 'active risk.' Active risk is not necessarily bad because there are some managers who are actually better than others, but in reality, they are few and are not always available but you can find them. If you decide to move away from the basic risk, you must be convinced that:

- Good managers exist

- That they are able to do better than their benchmark

- Above all, you must be capable of finding them!

If you were able to complete each of the three phases, it is appropriate to rely on active funds, otherwise, ETFs are preferred because they cost less and carry precisely where you decided to go, without additional surprises.

The techniques for choosing the ETF that best suits your investment strategies are different; an interesting methodology is applied to sector rotation is that the market as a whole is made up of different equity sectors, corresponding to the different economic sectors and their continuous alternation from the origin to the expansion and contraction phases. For this reason, the moments in which all the economic sectors grow or decrease simultaneously are quite rare.

The concept of sector rotation is useful in

order to identify, on one hand, the stage of maturity of the current primary trend and on the other to select those sectors that are growing relative to their strength. For example, sectors sensitive to changes in interest rates tend to anticipate both the minimums and the maximums of the market, while the sectors sensitive to the demand for capital goods or raw materials generally tend to follow the overall trend of the market with delay. Through ETFs, it is possible to take an immediate position on a specific stock market, without necessarily being forced to buy the different securities belonging to that particular basket. In this way, it is possible to obtain an immediate exposure on this sector, at the same time benefiting from its growth in value, besides the advantages linked to the diversification.

For example, if one thinks that at a given moment the US market should grow in relative terms to a greater extent than the French one, it will be appropriate to make the first one and to underweight the second one. This decision can be reached by analyzing the comparative relative strength between the two markets, which compares two dimensions (composed of market, sector, securities or other indices) to show how these values are performing in a relative manner and their respect for each other. The trend changes expressed by relative strength generally tend to anticipate the actual ones of the financial activity to which it refers. It is, therefore, possible to use the relative strength in order to direct purchases towards ETFs that show a growing relative force.

The great flexibility of ETFs also allows the construction of a guaranteed capital investment; in times of financial turbulence, investors often turn to products that provide capital protection which is those provided by financial intermediaries that often have high fees and charges for customers. Not many people know that it is possible to build a guaranteed capital product by yourself, which respects your personal investment needs! The central point of the logic of guaranteed capital is interest rates and the duration of the investment because at the base of all there are the two central concepts of finance:

- The higher the interest rates, the greater the return on the money

- As the duration increases, you earn more, because money 'works' longer

The money we will obtain in many years can be brought to today, as for bills that follow the discount law (the technical term of bringing the future money to today). You can easily answer the question: "To have 100 euros in seven years, knowing that the rates are at 5%, how much money do I have to invest?" This statement indicates how much money is needed to invest today to get the desired amount at maturity. The bonds that only allow the fruits to reach maturity, without paying interest during their life, are called zero-coupon bonds (ZCB) and are quite common on the market. If for example I want to have €100 at maturity and interest rates are at 5% I will have to invest in zero coupon bonds € 95.24 (if the deadline is between 1 year) € 78.35 (if the deadline is in 5 years) € 61.39 (if the deadline is 10 years) 48.1 € (if the deadline is between 15 years) and 23.21 € (if the deadline is 30 years)

In effect, by building an investment with guaranteed capital, one only has to decide how to invest the remaining part of the initial 100 euros that have not been allocated in the zero coupons. An ideal solution is to invest in options because, thanks to the leverage effect, they can amplify any yield. If you have an investment profile that's less than aggressive, ETFs are excellent tools to build a guaranteed capital investment. If, for example, we assume a 10-year investment with rates of 2.5% for that maturity, the portion to be invested in ZCB is equal to 78.12%, while the remaining 21.88% will be invested in ETF.

This investment strategy makes it possible to achieve a minimum (not real) 'money' return target with few operations, as the ZCB provides for the repayment only on the nominal amount of the loan (not discounted with the inflation rate). It is, therefore, a valid methodology for those who intend to make investments with clear objectives and have little time to devote to monitoring the values as only an operation until expiration is deemed necessary. Unlike a guaranteed capital product offered by any financial intermediary, an investment of this kind built independently with ETFs can be dismantled entirely or in pieces (selling only the ZCB or active assets, ETF) to meet any need. Naturally, only at maturity will there be a certainty of the pre-established return and, over the course of the loan, a temporary adverse trend in financial variables, (rates rise by lowering the ZCB and at the same time decreasing the value of the ETF) could result in the liquidation of losing positions. The same consequence would be selling a structured bond, with the advantage that 'doing it at home' the commissions are much lower and you can separate the two components and, if necessary, liquidate only one, according to your specific needs.

Conclusion

Thank you for making it through to the end of '*Swing Trading*: *The Ultimate Guide to Making Fast Money 1 Hour a Day*,' let's hope it was informative and that it was able to provide you with all of the tools you need to achieve your goals whatever they may be.

The next step is to start applying what you have learned during the course of this book and get started right away. Our suggestion is always to open up a demo account and make a few tries, before putting real money into it. Remember that you should never risk more than what you can afford to lose, so manage your capital wisely.

Finally, if you found this book useful in any way, a review on Amazon is always appreciated!

Swing Trading Strategies:

Learn How to Profit Fast With These 4 Simple Strategies

Table of Contents

Furthermore, the transmission, duplication or reproduction of any of the following work including specific information will be considered an illegal act irrespective of whether it is done electronically or in print. This extends to creating a secondary or tertiary copy of the work or a recorded copy and is only allowed with an express written consent from the Publisher. All additional rights reserved.

The information in the following pages is broadly considered to be a truthful and accurate account of facts and as such any inattention, use or misuse of the information in question by the reader will render any resulting actions solely under their purview. There are no scenarios in which the publisher or the original author of this work can be, in any fashion, deemed liable for any hardship or damages that may befall them after undertaking information described herein.

Additionally, the information in the following pages is intended only for informational purposes and should thus be thought of as universal. As befitting its nature, it is presented without assurance regarding its prolonged validity or interim quality. Trademarks are mentioned without written consent and can in no way be considered an endorsement from the trademark holder.

Introduction

Congratulations on downloading 'Swing Trading Strategies: Learn How to Profit Fast with These 4 Simple Strategies' and thank you for doing so.

Many people view swing trading as more of a fundamental approach to investing in the stock market. Unlike with day trading where positions are never held for more than a single day, swing traders can conceivably hold their positions for up to several days or even a week or more; some may even hold them for a month.

Still, this is not a clear picture of what swing trading actually is. It is a form of trading that sits right in the center of two other popular trading mechanisms, day trading, and trend trading. The day trader needs to make superfast decisions and may only hold his assets for a few seconds before selling. Trend traders, on the other hand, are usually in the market for the long haul. They could conceivably hold their trades for months at a time. Swing trading is a blend of these two very different trading styles.

To be successful as a swing trader, it is important to know how to choose the right stocks to invest in. Ideally, you'll want to look for large-cap stocks, which tend to be the most actively traded on most exchanges. In this book, you'll learn how to ride the waves in one direction and know when to get off and collect your rewards at the end.

In the following pages you'll learn:

- How to develop the mind of the trader

- The 'Sector Rotation' strategy

- How to use the 4-hour chart

- What to do with trading fakeouts

- How to execute momentum trading

There is a lot you can learn before you even get started. Keep in mind that no one knows everything there is to know about trading the markets so see this as your first book among many. Here we hope to lay the groundwork from which you can then catapult yourself into a whole new world of profits and hopefully to a whole new way of making a living. With that said, let's get started.

Happy Trading!
There are plenty of books on this subject on the market, so thanks again for

choosing this one! Every effort was made to ensure it is full of as much useful information as possible, please enjoy!

Chapter 1: The Mindset of a Trader

There is a good reason why trading is not for everyone. Statistics show that the majority of those who attempt a career in trading is not successful. This leaves us with a burning question...what is the cause of so many failures? Is it because they lack experience? Is it because of the intensity of the trade itself? Or is it because they don't have the right knowledge?

The answer is probably yes to all of those and the answer could also be no. Every day, thousands of traders enter the market; some win and some lose. We all know exactly what happens when we win and make a pretty good windfall but how we react when we lose is another matter entirely.

Ask yourself, what do you do when you lose or make a poor investment choice? Some people may get discouraged, blame their losses on the volatility of the market and declare it as a waste of time. Another may also get discouraged and want to quit but the next day they somehow find a renewed experience and are ready to try again. But the true trader will see the loss as a reason to ask more questions and do more research. Yes, they will be disappointed by their losses but rather than let that loss be a stumbling block, they will use it instead as a stepping-stone. They will view it as an opportunity to revisit their data, reevaluate their position and find out what went wrong. In essence, they will use it as a learning opportunity and see it as becoming a better trader in the future.

Yes, the loss may have been a result of a lack of knowledge, limited experience, or even just bad decisions but in a trader's mind, the reason for losing a trade is not as important as how they react to that loss.

To be able to do that, a good trader must learn how to keep their personal feelings completely out of the trading process. When you are emotional, it can taint your perspective of trading and affect your judgment. Traders must have an almost mechanical approach to every decision they make.

While all traders are in it for the money, the best ones are in it for the thrill of the game. They are not just following the charts to see whether they are going up or down but are equally interested in perfecting their skills of analysis with every decision they make. They view everything as a real learning process.

When you trade you must make decisions quickly and be willing to stick to them and follow through with everyone. Each time you look at the charts, graphs, stocks, and other data, you may have only seconds to decide to get in or out of the market, there is absolutely no time for emotional involvement.

This means you need to be mentally stable, but many would be surprised to learn that you also need to be in good physical condition as well. They do not understand that good physical conditioning can actually support your mental acuity. Eating well, getting good physical exercise, and maintaining healthy habits actually supports your mental faculties, which could easily impact your choices when it comes to making good trading decisions. People who have poor health may not realize how their physical condition could have an adverse effect on their decision-making process.

Trading is more than the ability to watch the numbers going up and down on a graph, it's about the psychology behind those numbers. All those squiggly lines, bars, and shapes represent decisions that individuals make to enhance their interest in a particular stock so the trader must have the ability to get into the minds of others and predict what he or she expects the majority of people will do. Then the trader needs to determine where he or she will best fit in that picture and make their decisions accordingly. At the same time, a trader must also create an escape hatch that will help them to get out of a trade to cut their losses whenever a decision he or she makes goes wrong.

The mind of the trader must be able to handle stress as well. It is difficult to watch the rise and fall of the market and realize that you missed your window to get in or out at the right time. One bad decision in this regard could really ruin your life in the future. It is said that patience is a virtue but it can also be a lifesaver for the true and most successful traders.

Just as you would work to hone your physical body, the best traders also put a lot of energy in developing their skills and sense of discipline. The more you practice in this area, the easier it will be. The ability to identify a good stock, learning how to time the market, and predicting price movements are just the public demonstration of the psychology behind the art of trading.

You also must be willing to be a lifelong learner. When it comes to navigating the many instruments you can trade in, you will always find that there is something else you need to learn. This means you must have humility and be willing to openly admit when you don't know something. The moment you become over-confident and think you've mastered a certain skill you can pretty much bet that something will come along to knock you back down a peg or two. You'll either lose your shirt or you'll be beating yourself up for a missed opportunity.

There is a very specific art to swing trading and learning everything you can about the market is tricky. Being able to do a proper analysis and make right decisions is only a reflection of what's going on in your own personal mindset. To be a good trader, one that is successful most of the time, depends on how well your mind works and how well you know and understand people. Every trade you make will be a reflection of that mental acuity that you have developed. If you for any reason feel that you are weak in this regard, don't despair. It just means that now is the time to start sharpening your tools so you're ready to get the best that you can possibly get out of your trades.

How to Find Potential Trades

One of the most important factors in successful trading is mastering the ability to choose the right instruments to trade. Many do not realize that there is also a certain psychology to making the right choice. It is just as important to identify not just those stocks that will move but also where to look for them. No matter how good you are at trading if you can't identify the right instruments to trade you won't get very far as a trader. You need to be able to identify those stocks that have enough movement to generate a profit for you and those that have the volume to match it.

When choosing a good trading stock it is not enough to pick something you just like and can get excited about but you must also be able to put your personal feelings aside and focus solely on the numbers.

While a good product is definitely a plus, much more is involved in choosing the right stock. You want to see more than movement, you must also be able to identify the direction its next move will be. To do this, you should look for those stocks that have a strong risk/reward ratio.

You can identify these stocks by the current news items circling around them, their numbers will show them usually moving up or down more than 2% even before the market opens, and they generally have a lot of unusual premarket activity to go along with it.

Keep in mind that not all stocks are ideally suited for trading so as a trader you will need to be willing to evaluate them on a case-by-case basis. Just because a stock has a high trade volume does not necessarily mean that it is a good choice for swing trading and the fact that it has a low trading volume does not preclude it from consideration. Only after careful analysis can you determine whether a stock is the ideal trading instrument. You need to look for those stocks that are performing outside of the average to decide if it's the right choice for you.

There are many factors that must be considered when trying to choose the right stock. It is easy to think that you can just go by the books and get the results you want but that would put you at a disadvantage. The numbers can reveal a great deal about a particular stock but sometimes just relying on your human instinct can be a better gauge for making the right choice or even knowing just

where you should look to find the right
stock for your next trade.

Making the right choice will depend on a
combination of your personal knowledge
of the market, the skills you have honed to
perfection and your natural instinct.
Missing any one of those factors could
definitely cause a major problem for
anyone looking to get into swing trading.

Chapter 2: The Sector Rotation Strategy

One of the most effective strategies in swing trading is sector rotation. It has been proven to be an excellent means of generating profits with the least amount of risk. There are a few things you must keep in mind when you're practicing sector rotation:

- Market Timing — when the market is going down avoid buying any stock. This includes purchasing any type of ETFs or sector funds.

- You will divide the market up into specific sectors. Some of these sectors will perform better at different times than at other times.

- Evaluation of each sector using both technical and fundamental analysis.

- Rotate the sectors every month to capitalize on your profit potential.

We'll go through each of these phases in more detail in the next section.

The general idea behind sector rotation is that each sector may perform differently depending on the time of the year it is. So, while some sectors may perform well in the spring others may have their time in the limelight in the summer or winter seasons.

Your goal is to identify those stocks and when you have the best chance of generating a profit from them. To do this, you will need to break down the different stocks into sectors first and do a detailed analysis of each sector. Once you've chosen the sector you want to trade in, you will have to do a separate analysis of each stock within that sector to narrow down your options for trading.

There are a number of websites that are perfect for listing the different sectors and the stocks contained in them. For a quick reference, you can go to Finviz.com to get a listing of the ones that are performing the best. However, if you are just beginning, it may be better for you to do the analysis and ranking yourself so that you can get a better feel for how they are divided up.

The general gist of sector rotation is being able to move your money from one industry to the next in an attempt to glean the most out of the market at any given time. As you go through the different industries, it is important to keep in mind that the past performance of any particular stock is not a guarantee of future success. With that thought in mind, there are four different stages of market movement you must understand.

- **Market Bottom:** This is the point where the prices of a particular stock begin to decline, creating an all-time low.

- **Bull Market:** This is when the market begins to rally and come back to life.

- **Market Top:** This is the point when the market reaches its maximum potential and begins to flatten out.

- **Bear Market:** This is when the market starts its long trip to the market bottom.

There are also four stages of the economic cycle that are important to always keep in mind. Remember that these cycles usually trail behind the market cycles by at least a few months.

Full Recession

When there is a full recession, it can be a difficult time for many businesses. The country's GDP will have been retracting for several quarters, interest rates will have dropped, and consumer expectations will have seriously declined. There are few industries that fare well during this period of time, however, those that are cyclical tend to do better. The technological industry and industrial markets also seem to do well in this type of economic climate.

Early Recovery

In this phase, things are beginning to improve economically. Consumers will begin to expect more from the market and industrial production is starting to see a gradual increase. By this time, interest rates have already bottomed out and aren't expected to fall any further, and the yield curve (the line that plots the interest rates used as a benchmark for measuring the economic climate) is starting to rise. Industries that tend to do better in this type of economic cycle are usually the industrial sector, those that supply basic materials, and towards the end of this cycle, you might even see potential in the energy sector.

Late Recovery

During this economic phase, you will see a rapid increase in interest rates and the yield curve will begin to flatten out. Consumer expectations will begin to drop and the industrial industry will level off. Industries that fare better during this phase include energy, staples, and services.

Early Recession

During the early recession, things will begin to decline for everyone. This is a period when consumer expectations will fall to an all-time low, the production industry will start to fall, and interest rates will be at their highest. The yield curve will neither be rising or falling but instead will remain flat or maybe inverted. The industries most likely to perform well in this economic climate will be services, utilities, cyclical, and transports.

In most situations, financial markets will try to predict the economic climate in the future. They may make predictions as far ahead as six months, putting the market cycle ahead of the economic cycle. So, when you hear news reports about the economic condition of a particular stock it may be well ahead of the current situation. So, a stock may be struggling at the time but the news reports may already be talking about its recovery.

This gives you a pretty basic understanding of how the different sectors can be divided up and how to choose which ones will be best suited to trade. Even with this basic overview, you can quickly determine which industries are most likely to succeed during the different stages of the economic cycle. Once you've determined which market cycle and economic cycle you're in, it will be much easier to determine which companies you are more likely to take a risk on and give you a better chance at earning a profit.

There are two different ways you can earn profit through sector rotation. First, you can buy when the sector is trending upward and sell when the trend is beginning to fall backward. This is a basic rule of thumb, buy low and sell high. This concept is pretty easy to understand but it is not always easy to detect. If you're like most people who enter the market, deciding when a price has hit its peak so you know when to get out is not always easy. The same can be said for determining the point at which the price has hit its lowest point possible.

If you're not completely sure how to go about it, there are several free websites you can refer to that will give you their viewpoint on whether the price is maxed out or not. Whatever you do, it is not a good idea to guess at what stock will perform well. Flash crashes are quite common and to be forewarned is to be forearmed.

You can also use charts to predict market movements. Beginners usually will start with something simple like the Simple Moving Average (SMA) to help them to make their decisions. Listed below are a few ways you can use to help you decide which way to go.

Identifying the Bottom of a Sector

It is difficult to determine when a sector has reached the bottom or the top of its cycle. However, if you choose to use the SMA-350, (that's the Single Moving Average over 350 sessions) to determine the market you could probably get a pretty good picture of when the market will begin to make its next dive.

Historically, stock prices have generally been seen to hit bottom after six months into a recession. As we've already pointed out, once several quarters have closed the negative growth of the GDP is a strong indicator. However, identifying these periods is not always that easy to see. Usually, if you rely on the six-month in a pattern most of the action has already taken place. As the expression goes, hindsight is always 20/20. However, there are other strategies that can actually be very useful when it comes to detecting a bottomed out stock.

Nothing could be better than getting into the market when a stock has reached its bottom point. That's when you can buy at the lowest possible prices and then ride the wave all the way to the top. To do that, you just have to watch and observe the averages before it reaches that point. If the averages have experienced a large break that falls below the previous low, it is a signal that you need to follow that stock and observe what happens next. There are several things that can happen. If the average experiences some type of reversal it could be an indication that a double bottom is developing.

You can also keep a close eye on the stock's volume. This measures the amount of activity going on with that stock; which is basically how much buying and selling is actually happening. If you observe a heavy volume going either up or down it is an indication that the buyers and sellers have a pretty strong conviction. If there is a lot of volume moving up then there is strong support from buyers and if you see a lot of volume moving down it indicates that there is a great deal of support from sellers.

Looking at economic numbers can also tell you a great deal about a stock. The market will experience a decline after negative news reports appear in the media. You need to think of the press as a reflection of the psychology of the moment. When you begin to see repeated headlines discussing how bad the economy has become, it is usually a sign that the majority of people have developed a very negative attitude towards the market and many investors will be moving out of their positions running for a safer haven as a result.

Consumer Confidence Index

Right after the market has bottomed out, consumer spending will begin to increase showing that consumer confidence has improved. This can be observed when they begin to spend more money and businesses start to see an increase in their earnings.

Managers' Index

This measures the economic health of a sector. When the consumer's confidence index and the manager's index both have hit rock bottom they will begin a steady rise that will continue for several months. You'll usually see this when you're observing the movements of the manufacturing and service sectors and indicates that they are beginning to expand and grow again.

High Yield Bonds

The high yield bond spread consists of bonds from companies who are at a high risk of default. To draw investors that they can borrow from, they will offer to pay a higher interest rate as an incentive. When the usual lending standards begin to relax you will notice the amount of interest for these types of loans will start to drop. This is a sign that banks and other financial institutions are prepared to take on more risk showing that the economic conditions are beginning to improve.

Copper Prices

Many will also look at how the price of copper is moving. It is usually a good measure when showing the strength or weakness of the overall economy. Since copper is so widely used in products like pipes, radiators, electronics, and other technological devices, observing how its price moves is a pretty good measure in determining consumer demand. If you notice that the price has bottomed out then you can pretty much determine that the demand for those products is also pretty low. However, if there is still room for the price to drop further it's a good chance that there is still some demand for the production of many of the products that use copper.

Ideally, you want to enter the market when the prices have reached the bottom and are starting to climb upward again. It means that there is an increase in demand and prices are about to rise once more.

Being able to identify a market bottom is a key factor for any trader. It requires looking at a variety of different factors that involve both technical analyses as well as understanding the psychology of the masses. You could choose to rely entirely on the numbers but you would only be cheating yourself. However, when you use all the different indicators you can unlock the key to a host of profit potential.

Detecting the Trend

Another strategy you can use in sector rotation is detecting the trend. Sometimes this can be much easier than identifying the top or the bottom of a market cycle. Some traders use the metric SME-50 (50-day Single Moving Average). Here if you see the stock price has moved up more than 3% above the SMA-50 it is a good time to buy in, but if you see the price has dropped more than 3% below the SMA-50 that's when it is a good idea to sell.

Of course, once you get the hang of this type of analysis, you can always adjust your metric. You don't need to stick to the 3% threshold and may prefer to use 1% or 2%. The key is to find a measure that will work best for you. Generally, if you plan to hold your stocks for a longer period of time, it is better to use a higher percentage and if you plan to sell after only a short period of time, use a lower percentage. You should also adjust your formula to reflect the frequency of the trades you want to make as well.

Identifying market crashes is also important. This tells you when it's a good time to get back into the market. There are also several indicators to help you to determine this as well.

The RSI (14) is a measure showing whether or not a stock has been overbought or oversold. The RSI usually oscillates between 0 – 100. A stock is considered to be overbought when the value increases to above 70 and it is oversold if the measured value is below 30.

What Should You Buy

Now that you have a good idea of when to get into the market and the type of market you want to trade you're only halfway there. In each industry, there may be hundreds if not thousands of stocks to choose from so narrowing down your search to a good stock can be a little tricky. The stocks you choose will depend on a number of varying factors, some may be within your control and others may be out of your powers of influence.

You will have to consider your level of experience, and the amount of capital you want to invest. The method you chose to try to pick your stocks should be a part of your permanent trading plan and should be adjusted as your experience and knowledge in this field grows. Keep in mind that stocks will have different levels of price movements and velocity. Some will move very slowly and others will move very quickly. All of these factors will help you to decide which is the best choice for you.

Before you even begin to choose stocks, however, it is important for you to determine the kind of risk exposure you can handle. Your strategy should be created with this foremost in mind. You want to reduce the amount of capital at risk and limit your exposure but at the same time, you want to earn a sizable profit. The best way to accomplish that is to make enough right decisions that you can generate a steady stream of profit for yourself.

Keep your process simple. Whatever strategy it is that you're using start by trading a single stock and then sit back and observe what happens. Every stock has its own personality and habits. The more you understand them the easier it will be to anticipate its movements. Look at the charts at different times throughout the day to determine when it moves and how it responds to external stimuli. Think of it as developing a love interest. You want to know all its little quirks and habits. In time, your relationship will solidify and you'll be able to predict its movements with surprising accuracy. You won't get it right every time but the number of wrong predictions will eventually begin to diminish. Once you've reached a level of consistency, you can move on to get to know other stocks in your particular industry.

One important thing you need to remember. Once you've started a trading plan, do not change it while you have a stock in play. Once you've pulled out and the market is closed, you can then look back and make some adjustments to your plan. This way you will know the exact results of your decision and you'll get a clearer picture of whether or not your trading strategy is really working or not.

For the beginning, an investor should remember these basic guidelines.

- Pick a maximum of 50 stocks to trade but invest them 1 at a time until they become second nature to you

- Choose the low stock prices but not at the bottom, make sure they are at least above the $25 range

- Look for an average 30-day volume that is higher than 500,000 shares per day

- 25 of your shares should be set aside for long investments

    o They should show increasing revenues and earnings
    o Have a strong presence in their sectors
    o Have a moving average around 200
    o Could even be following S&P Futures

- 25 of your shares should be used for short-term investments

    - These should show declining revenues and earnings
    - Have a weak presence in their sectors
    - Have a moving average below 200
    - Could be following S&P Futures

Some Sectors That Have Been Favorable for Swing Traders

- Retailing

- Automotive

- Housing

These industries usually suffer when the interest rates are very high, however, when the economy begins to improve these industries will quickly recover.

You can also look at sectors based on the economy. Those in foreign countries will respond to different factors. You will have to consider currency fluctuations, political climate, and favorable or unfavorable events in the news.

When to Rotate

Once you have your sector choices for the market timing, you will need to know when to get out and switch to another sector. There are several methods to help you to decide exactly when it's the best time to rotate.

- When the market is on a downward slope

- When the fundamentals of your chosen sector start to go bad

- When you can find another sector with a higher potential for appreciation

- When you see that the sector is peaking and has met your target objectives

Top-Down Investing

With top-down investing the approach is a little different. You must look at the overall economy and then break down each of its components into smaller details. This means getting a good look at the global world scene, you can examine the different industrial sectors and choose those that have the potential of outperforming the market.

To do this you can use the macroeconomic variables like the trade balances, GDP, currency movements, inflation, and interest rates to help you to narrow down which sectors are most likely to be high performing.

Many investors get this information from hosted forums like the UBS CIO Global Forum held in Beverly Hills, California in 2016 to help them navigate the current economic environment. These venues address many of the macroeconomic factors that investors need to know. Open discussions on international governments, central banking, differing monetary policies, and what's happening in international companies can all have an influence on how a sector is responding in the market.

List of Sectors You Might Want to Consider

- Consumer Discretionary

- Consumer Staples

- Energy

- Financial (including banks, insurances, and brokers)

- Health Care (including pharmaceuticals)

- Industrial

- Material

- Technology

- Utilities

- Automotive

Each of these sectors can be subdivided into even smaller sector groups.

Now that you have all of your information together, you can now narrow down your search and determine which sectors you will trade in when you plan to trade, and which stocks you will focus the majority of your interest in. Sector rotation sounds very simple here but there are many factors that must be considered if you want to make this type of investment strategy profitable for you.

Chapter 3: The 4-Hour Chart

Using the 4-hour chart is another popular method often used by swing traders. There are quite a few good reasons why working with this chart is so appealing. First, it is a bit longer than the smaller 5-minute or 15-minute charts that do not give a full enough picture of what's really happening with the money. But it is just long enough for investors to get a pretty good picture of what's kind of movement is going on in the market. By using this type of chart, it is pretty easy to see just who is in control at any given time, the bears or the bulls.

With the 4-hour chart strategy, the idea is to tap into the prevailing trends and make the most out of them by using a combination of several different moving averages, support or resistance, volatility, and other tools. When used together, these can help you to maximize your profits while at the same time keep your losses down to a minimum.

With the 4-hour chart as your base, you can screen for potential areas where you might find trading signals. Your main goal here is to identify either an uptrend or a downtrend and then follow its unique behavior.

This is usually done by using two different sets of moving averages; one will be a 34 period and the other will be based on the 55 periods. These are both numbers that can be found in the Fibonacci sequence. You will be able to determine if a trend is good for trading or not by analyzing the relationship between the price action and the moving averages.

To Determine the Uptrend

You will be able to identify an uptrend if you have observed any of the following conditions

- The price actions are higher than the two moving averages

- The price action remains above both moving averages

- If the 34 moving average is higher than the 55 moving average and remains high

- If the moving averages are sloping upward for the majority of the time on the chart

To Identify a Downtrend

For there to be a downtrend, the same conditions must be observed but in the opposite direction.

- When the price action falls below the two moving averages

- The price action stays below the two moving averages

- The 34 moving average is lower than the 55 moving average and remains low

- The moving averages are on a downward slope for the majority of the time and continue to fall behind the trend

Your goal is to profit on the swings that follow in the direction of the trend. This means you must also look for retracements and enter the market at that point. Below are some basic guidelines that can help you to decide the best point to enter the market.

- A trend must be identified in the 4th hour with the moving averages meeting the criteria listed above.

- Wait for a retracement to begin and then watch for the price to move in the direction of the two moving averages.

- When you see the retracement has reached the area between the two moving averages, look at the 1-hour chart of possible entry points.

- Find the retracement trendline that is moving counter to the trend and has touched the trend line at least three times.

- In the 1-hour chart, look for a breakout where a retracement trendline has closed in the same direction as the larger trend.

- Enter when the breakout price closes past the trendline.

One of the advantages of this strategy is that the trends are much more easily identified on the 4-hour chart. In most charts the upswings will be seen with white, rising candles and downswings can be seen with black, falling candles. It should be pretty easy to see the difference.

As a swing trader, you need to be able to visualize these movements and compare them to the current market situation. This strategy works best when there is an up or down trend but will work even when there is a sideways trend.

There is a bit of psychology involved this trading strategy too. When the market experiences a certain level of support, there are many buyers hanging on the sidelines just waiting to jump in at the moment it moves up or down. As a trader, it is important that you can identify the psychological marks and predict when others are prepared to join the party.

Timing

The 4-hour chart also makes it easier to figure out the right time to enter or exit the market. When it comes to swing trading, in addition to getting the direction right you need to know when is the optimum time to get in or out. As a matter of fact, timing plays a major factor in how well you do.

You also need to be concerned about periodic counter movements. At times you'll notice the market may run as much as 30-50 points against your position, but you will still make a profit if you stay your course. This is one advantage that a swing trader has over a day trader, who could never afford those types of counter movements.

Swing traders can also turn a much larger profit for each position they take. Chances are you are more likely to gain the most profit from those unexpected movements rather than those you predicted. With this method, you will typically have several hours to decide on a specific entry point so you can afford to wait until you've found the perfect time to take your position.

Setting your Stop-Loss Placement

While this is a very profitable way to make money with swing trading, it is not without risks. Therefore, it is very important that each time you set your position you also create your own stop-loss placement carefully. This will help you to reduce your exposure to risk and keep you from bleeding money when things go wrong.

Stop-loss placement is not the most idealistic decision a swing trader needs to make but is likely the smartest. If you do not fully understand how to pick the right position to stop your losses you stand to suffer considerable consequences. It is the single most powerful weapon needed to manage your risks.

The general theory is that the stop-loss should be based on a specific level in the market. The price action should have breached that level as evidence that your trade was actually wrong. Ideally, you want to see that the price has actually invalidated your view and has used fact-based evidence as proof in the form of a breach of support or resistance.

There are several different types of stop-losses you can put into place. They are there as a protection not just from you losing but to help you to be aware of potential losing trades. There is a tendency, especially among new traders to hold onto losing trades for far too long. We see a price plunging and it is just human nature to hold onto them in hopes that they will rebound, no matter what the conditions really are. By having a stop loss in place, it reduces your exposure to risk and cuts your losses.

Before you can accurately place a stop-loss, you must first answer one question: "At what point is it determined that your trade is wrong?" To answer this you will need to go back to your analysis, which will tell you not only determine where to place your stop-loss but also what type of stop-loss you will need.

Hard Stop

This is the easiest stop-loss placement you can use. It is just a matter of placing a stop at a certain number of pips from your entry price. A pip is actually the smallest price movement that any exchange can make. So, if a price is set at four decimal places, the smallest change would be that of the last decimal point or $1/100^{th}$ of 1%. This means that you must also factor in the actual movement in the market. More volatile markets will require larger pips to be effective and less volatile markets will require a smaller number of pips to show that your decision may have been wrong.

Average True Range % Stop

Another type is the ATR% stop, which can be used in any type of market. It is often used to determine the average true range of a particular stock. This range measures the volatility of a stock over a set period of time. When the ATR is higher, it is an indication of a more volatile market but a lower ATR shows less volatility. Using this measure to determine your stop point is a way of ensuring that your stop will not be static but will be dynamic enough to change with the prevailing market conditions.

Multiple Day High/Low

This type of stop is a popular one for swing traders. When taking a long position, the stop would be placed at the point where the trader will expect the day's low to be. This will allow you to exit the position at the first point where the break below that point is reached.

Closes Above or Below Price Levels

You can also set your stops when the price closes above or below predetermined price levels. With this type of stop, there is no actual stop placed in your trading software, instead, you will have to close it manually when it reaches a specific point.

Which Markets are Best?

When it comes to swing trading there are certain markets that are much better with the 4-hour chart than others. Shares may be the first choice but they are not always the most ideal for all traders. There are certain factors that are out of your control that can impact your ability to earn a profit.

For those traders that wish to avoid huge price gaps, the alternative is to trade in specific markets. Rather than focus on particular stocks to invest in, concentrate on a market as a whole. For example, for those who choose to trade the Dow Jones, they are investing in not a single stock but in 30 different companies. So, while a single share may struggle on a particular day it is much more difficult for the entire market to experience a major loss.

This will prevent there being extreme gaps in profit earnings when the markets are very volatile. It is important to point out that there is no guarantee that this strategy won't experience major losses; it simply lowers your overall risk of losses you might experience by focusing your energies on a single stock. So, which markets are the best?

Indices
Bonds

Currencies

When you focus your attention on these, you will see many correlations that you can gauge by following practical rules. For example,

- When the American markets start to rise, markets in the other parts of the world will also see an increase.

- If the US dollar sees an increase, other currencies will often go down

- When the dollar is strong, other commodities are often weakened.

Simply by following these basic rules, you are fully prepared to know when to enter and exit the market and what to expect.

Which Instruments Are Best for Swing Trading?

Exchange-traded funds are investment funds that are traded on an exchange. Even if you don't know anything about these ETFs, there is plenty of information online so you can learn about the pretty quickly.

The majority of ETF's have a pretty good liquidity so it should be relatively easy to sell your position when you are ready to exit. Some of the most popular ETFs include SPT – Standard and Poor's 500, QQQ – NASDAQ, and GLD – Gold.

When you trade on the 4-hour chart you need to develop a good understanding of the different items that you come across when you do your analysis. While you may have already heard of some of these expressions, it is a good idea to review them again so that you start off on the right foot. When you are searching for a setup (a pattern found on the stock market chart) you need to know what each of these things means. Many of them are very simple and basic but it helps to understand them when you see them and use them in making your investment decisions.

Support and Resistance

Look for support and resistance. These are some of the most powerful characteristics you can find when you're analyzing a market chart. These are usually found when you are doing your technical analysis.

Support is found when a price level appears at the point where the market repeatedly turns upward. This is the point when buyer interest increases. The more buyers in a market the higher the price will be.

Resistance is just the opposite. It is the point when the price level turns downward indicating that there are more sellers in the market. These push the prices down.

The reason why these points are so crucial is that, in some markets, a larger investor will only buy in when the price hits a certain point. While we can't all manipulate the market like this, knowing when these points happen can help you to buy in at the same point and reap the same profits.

As a swing trader, being able to recognize these pivot points could be one of the most profitable strategies you can have at your disposal. It will allow you to buy at

the support level and sell at the resistance
level for a steady stream of income.

Double Top and Double Bottom

Another pattern you will see on the charts is the double top and the double bottom. The double top pattern can usually be identified by an 'M' on the chart. It is viewed as an indication of an intermediate or sometimes a long-term price reversal. There will be two bullish attempts to push the price up past the resistance levels with two failed attempts to break through the threshold.

This pattern usually appears at the end of a long and extended uptrend. After reaching a specific high, the price will make a significant drop in value and create a trough before another attempt to break through to the new high. The second peak appears to be reaching the first peak but is usually with a lower volume of trade. It's a sign that the bulls have lost confidence in the fight. The price drops again and the bears will take control.

This is considered to be a bearish chart pattern and is confirmed only when the price breaks at the low point of the trough. Traders can find this by looking for a high volume breakdown and then enter with a short position to take advantage of the reversal.

Ideally, you want to calculate the distance between the two peaks and the trough and then subtract the result from the lowest point of the trough to find the right point of entry for your trade.

The double bottom pattern is exactly the opposite and can be recognized as a 'W' on the charts. It gives you a good picture of a drop in a particular stock, then an attempt to rebound, followed by another drop to almost the same point before it rebounds a second time.

To trade on a double bottom, the closing price can be found on the second rebound and is almost to the previous high of the first rebound. You'll see an increase in volume combined with fundamentals that give evidence that the market conditions are in agreement with the reversal. Trade long in this environment and enter at the top of the price point of the first rebound and set your stop at the second low.

The best way to trade on a double bottom is to stay abreast of the kind of news that would influence your stock. The more you know about what's going on and what factors are influencing buyer's decisions is to keep on top of the media and make sure that you know what's about to happen before it actually does.

Breakouts

Another pattern you need to be able to identify are the breakouts. These occur when the price moves outside of the support and resistance levels along with a large increase in volume. Those who trade on a breakout position usually enter long right after the stock price breaks above the resistance level. They can enter a short position when the price breaks below the support.

It is important to note that once a breakout occurs volatility tends to increase as the price is moving beyond a known parameter. Breakouts are found in all types of markets and generally represent the most explosive price movements.

When trading on a breakout, keep in mind the support and resistance levels. The more times a stock price has touched on these areas, the stronger these levels become. That means that the longer these areas have been at work, the better the result will be when the price finally breaks.

Choosing your entry point is pretty basic when you're trading with a breakout. Once the price is set to close above the resistance level, you can take a bullish position and when it closes below the support level you can take a bearish position.

Flags

Once a trend movement becomes strong you will begin to see consolidation on the chart. The market will seem like it has stalled for a short period of time and then it will continue on following the prevailing trend. Sometimes this lack of movement is referred to as a 'trend continuation pattern.' It looks sort of like a flag on the charts with the previous uptrend forming the pole and the short bursts of consolidation taking the shape of the flag.

When a flag formation is reached, traders can speculate on whether or not the trend will continue. These are great opportunities for a trader to speculate on both sides. There are bullish as well as bearish flags so there is an opportunity on both sides.

If you can play the flags just right, you can typically earn a pretty good risk-reward ratio. These appear frequently on the 4-hour chart, which makes it the perfect tool to use with this strategy.

Chapter 4: Trading Fakeouts

There is no doubt that talking about the market is much easier than actually doing it. With so many factors to consider it's no wonder that many people end up giving up after a time. Every trader needs their own body of algorithms, formulas, and strategies to help them navigate the sometimes murky waters of the trading game.

Those new to trading may be surprised to discover that everything you see on a chart is not always as it appears. There are often tricky characteristics that have been manipulated without the best of intentions. These are sometimes referred to as 'fakeouts' or 'feints.' Being able to identify them can be instrumental in helping you to avoid pitfalls and dangers that can easily overtake a newcomer and leave you helpless.

It is true that the same patterns on charts are repeated over and over again. These can usually be identified when you perform a technical analysis but even then it may not always be clear.

To avoid being caught in a fakeout it helps to get a clear understanding of what it is. A fakeout (feint) can be described as a situation where the trader takes a position in anticipation of an expected price movement, but that movement never actually happens. Instead, the asset moves opposite of the trader's position.

To avoid this happening, it is recommended that you always use more than one indicator when making trading decisions. As you gain more experience in trading, you'll find that those traders who are most successful even rely on four or more indicators before they commit to a decision.

How to Spot a Fakeout

These fakeouts can occur anywhere, at any time, and in all types of markets so it pays to know just how to spot them when they appear. Below is a list of tips that can help even the beginning trader to identify fakeouts and avoid them.

One of the best ways to identify a true fakeout is by studying the charts of legitimate trends so you can learn how to recognize how price movements really do develop. You'll be able to see this in the candlestick pattern on the chart.

If there is a sudden rise in the market, you should be able to identify only white candles on the chart. Black candles appear when there is a downtrend. In these markets, you'll find that there is a loyal following. With these types of stocks, it is pretty easy to predict movements so it won't be easy for a large trader to get in and manipulate the prices.

Once the trend has reached its target, the market generally calms down and the volatility decreases. After that, it moves sideways for a period of time. It appears to be meandering aimlessly without forming any clear direction as if it were resting. In this scenario, all traders seem to have come to an agreement on the expected price point.

This scenario usually occurs when there is an expectation of big news relating to the stock. Reports of labor market disputes, major economic changes, or interest rate adjustments can often have a big impact on how the market will perform. It is the trader's responsibility to identify the validity of the movements and if he should anticipate more movement in a specific direction. However, if there is nothing happening in the market, no big news reports on the horizon, or no other indication of a change in price, you should probably assume it is a fakeout.

Traders can manipulate markets easier when there is not a lot of volume going on. They understand that there are many people sitting on the sidelines waiting for a signal for them to jump in and if he has enough money he can set up a fakeout pretty easily and then he can come in and reap the benefits.

By setting up a breakout, for example, traders will easily jump into the fray anticipating a rise in price. However, the trader who initiated the breakout immediately reverses his position once the other traders have joined in, forcing them to close their positions with a loss.

To gain from being trapped in a fakeout, it is better to wait for a breakout and if it ends up being a feint, respond in the opposite direction. Fakeouts usually appear at the support and resistance levels so you should be able to identify and predict certain price movements. Many traders are often caught at this point as it is a common rule of thumb to buy at support levels and sell at resistance levels.

Trading the Fakeout

Once you know how to identify a fakeout, you should prepare a strategy that will allow you to make the most out of the experience. This is what more experienced traders do. Rather than accept a loss as newbies often do, by applying a few basic rules you can turn that potential loss into a possibility for profit.

- Find the consolidation zones in your chart so you can determine the range the price is moving in.

- Draw trend lines on the chart so that they are more visible. Look for a minimum of two contacts with the trend line.

- Avoid this range and wait, hold your position until you see if the breakout is successful or not. If it fails, it is a fakeout.

- If it is a fakeout, open behind the breakout but in the opposite direction. If the closing price still falls outside of the range, hold your position. It could turn out to be a successful breakout.

- Look for range support for the price target when making short trades. Look for range resistance if you're planning on making long trades.

- Make sure you place your stops above or below the fake candle to prevent major losses.

- Aim for a 1:2 ratio. For example, if the distance to the stop is 50 pips, your target price should be twice that.

Identifying Patterns

Fakeouts can appear in a variety of patterns and can be found in all kinds of market situations. You can usually spot them on technical chart points because those that create them are well aware of the number of investors looking for those points to establish entry positions. As a trader, you need to be able to spot these quickly to avoid getting caught in the trap. If you are smart and can make good decisions, you can do quite well if you follow the pattern of those sharks and reap some of their spoils in the process.

Flags

Technical analysts prefer to create this pattern with two trend lines keeping the small consolidation period contained in a narrow channel. The normal reaction is to expect the trend to move upwards, which would happen at the break of an upper channel line giving traders the buy signal to start another wave upward.

But with a fakeout, the opposite will happen first, triggering a sell signal. This will cause a slip in the price rather than an increase trapping those who were following the trend just a little too closely.

The smart trader will come in at a very low price and create a better risk-reward ratio, by monitoring this development more closely a nice windfall will be created for him or her.

Triangles

Triangles are another pattern you might observe a fakeout in. Normally, triangles are part of a continuation pattern where the analyst expects a breakout in the same direction as the trend. With a triangle fakeout, a swing trader could take a short position.

Market participants would expect the triangle to be a continuation of the trend and that it would resolve downward. They would assume that there was a start of an upward breakout, which would be a mistake. You will be able to identify this trick the moment the price appears to move in the wrong direction.

Channels

Channels are another way to create a fakeout on the charts. After the analyst has identified a trend he will look for a parallel trend line and connect the highs. Traders will naturally place their stops above the upper line if they plan to trade short or below the support line if they plan to trade long. Top traders are already aware of this move and will place large orders that will perform in the opposite direction of the intended trend. If they can get over the top, they push the prices upward and will keep pushing until their short orders are executed, thus creating a flood of sell orders. This will force the price back down and back into the channel. The best traders should recognize this move and follow suit, adding to the trend.

As a trader, make sure you wait for the actual fakeout before you get in. It's a good idea to wait until the stops have all been fished out before you enter your position in the channel. This will give you a stronger confirmation as long as you trade in the same direction of the fakeout.

Chapter 5: Momentum Trading

Momentum traders look for acceleration at a stock's price before they enter the market. Once they have identified the momentum, they will take their entry positions with the expectation that the momentum is going to continue to follow that trend. Their method of trade is very similar to those who trade trend channels but momentum traders are more likely to base their decision on short-term movements rather than on the fundamentals. This type of trading is not always easy and for that reason is more likely to be practiced by more experienced traders.

Timing is a key factor when you're momentum trading. Traders will set their entry points based on the speed of the stock movements and for that reason are much more interested in what's happening in the news at any given point in time. They look for those stocks that are moving high volumes in reaction to such reports.

To be a momentum trader you have to have a keen sense of concentration and have the ability to stick with it until the target has been reached. Those who are not disciplined enough will usually lose out in this type of trade. The moves often happen very quickly and their timing has to be absolutely spot-on.

Screening Stocks for Momentum Trading

When looking for potential trades your focus should be placed on the search for trends. Once you find the trends, look to see if there is a strong movement in a specific direction. These movements must be accompanied by a high volume and have lasted over an extended period of time. There are several ways to find these types of trends.

Some traders look at daily watch lists or are continuously monitoring news reports, message boards, or brokerage apps for the latest news that will trigger a high volume trend.

They will look at stock volume as well. Since their interest lies in the momentum of a trade, the volume will be a major factor to consider. If they notice more buyers than sellers in the market, the price will rise and more trading will happen.

They will look closely at resistance levels. After they identify the stock trend and its direction, they will search out stocks that are already testing their resistance levels. If they find one that breaks the resistance it is considered a good candidate for momentum trading.

Technical indicators can also help to identify a break in resistance. Momentum traders are more concerned with moves based on a price trend if the stock has passed its point of resistance rather than the traditional buy at the bottom and sell at the top strategy. Once they enter they will stay in the trade until they have reached their target profit amount or hit their stop-loss point.

Short Squeeze

A well-played short squeeze can give an investor quite a bit of profit. Investors look for heavily shorted stocks so they can maximize their potential for gains.

A short squeeze happens when a stock has a high proportion of short interest as opposed to the overall float. When the value of a stock that is heavily shorted begins to increase, anyone who is trading short starts to lose a substantial amount of money. To cover his position, the investor will have to buy shares in the marketplace. Normally, this action won't have an impact on the price unless there is an excessive amount of short interest in the stock. When that happens, the stocks become flooded with too many of these purchases. The knee-jerk reaction of most traders is their stop-loss positions. These investors will switch positions to become long, pushing the stock price even further along forcing more short positions to close.

Another great way to identify a potential short squeeze is by looking for opportunities to play one. These can be seen when there is a large short percentage of float. One of the best places to look for these is on the NASDAQ. The higher the interest in the 'short' the greater the potential.

You can also check the daily volume. Once you are pretty sure that you know the number of shares being traded on an average day, look for some of the benchmarks that indicate an above average volume of movement in the stock. Take the short interest and divide it by the average daily volume. When there is a higher value for the number of days it is usually an indication that it is a longer squeeze in play.

When you are ready to trade in, ensure that the price is on an upward trend with a bullish push behind it. When everything falls into place, and you are in a long position, ride the wave looking for signs of a pullback.

In this type of trade, it is important to watch the chart closely. Look for the same trends you found when you identified the squeeze but moving in the opposite direction. The volume will begin to spike as the price runs up after people begin to vacate their short positions. This would be a perfect example of watching a short squeeze as it plays out.

Conclusion

Thank you for making it through to the end of '*Swing Trading Strategies: Learn How to Profit Fast With These 4 Simple Strategies*,' let's hope it was informative and able to provide you with all of the tools you need to achieve your goals whatever it may be.

There are many ways one can invest in the stock market but swing trading seems to be one of the most popular. It doesn't have all the stress of the day trader and you have the ability to take your time as you navigate the market. This could be a very valuable tool when it comes to learning how to trade on the stock market.

The good news is that while in this book, we spent the majority of our time focusing on stocks, the techniques and strategies included here can easily be used in other areas as well. So, whether you prefer to invest in the Forex, currencies, or even cryptocurrencies, the charts, and graphs referred to can all be analyzed in a very similar way.

Even though this book is contained in a very small package there is a lot of information here. It is not likely you will remember it all in one passing so keep it near you as you begin to navigate the market and use it as a reference from time to time. You can also enhance your learning by doing additional research on reputable sites online. No one knows everything there is to know about trading so if you decide to pursue this course of action, remember that you will always be a student.

Still, with the right attitude and diligent application of these strategies, you'll find you will enter the market with a little more confidence than before. As you start, make sure that you start with small trades first and build up from there. With each success, I'm sure you'll be eager to try more and more but remember to exercise patience and don't go too deep in the waters until you're sure you can actually pull yourself back to shore when you need to just in case.

Always remember that stock trading is, by its nature, a highly risky venture where you are always in jeopardy of losing everything you put into it. Take your time and be sure about every move you make. Never enter the market without at least two ways to get out of it. Remember to leave your emotions at the door and simply follow the numbers, graphs, and charts and you'll end up trading with nerves of steel that will carry you a long way as a trader who practices swing trading.

Finally, if you found this book useful in any way, a review on Amazon is always appreciated!